Who am I?

Dominique Diender

BookLeaf Publishing

India | USA | UK

Presentation by *BookLeaf Publishing*

Web: www.bookleafpub.com

E-mail: info@bookleafpub.com

ISBN : 9789357447249

First edition 2021

DEDICATION

I dedicate this to the ones who need it.

I love you.

I do.

ACKNOWLEDGEMENT

I have to acknowledge that I have no idea what I am doing but I am doing it.

PREFACE

Before there was once upon a time there was a
dont tell anyone.

The leap of faith

I am the writer of my own story.
I am the paper. I am the pen.
All of the frustration and the glory.
I am the start. I am the end.

I am all of the blank pages,
that are waiting for the script.
I am the dream. I am the believer.
Just waiting for an idea to sink in.

I am the diver of my ocean.
I am the sea, the sky & the land.
I am the painter. I am the canvas.
I am the place where it never began

The baby

I am the child. I am the mother.
I am life and I am death.
I am the layers of my being.
I am the soul within my breath

I am joy, pleasure, laughter & happiness.
I am innocent. I am pure.
I am that beautiful smile on your face.
I am free and I am whole.

I am the art of his creation.
A true expression of the light
I am a diamond made from pressure
I am the moon who guards the night

The beat

I am the singer. I am the song.
I am the music, the floor and the dance.
I am the Queen. I am the throne.
I am the one who was given a chance.

I am the drum. I am the journey.
I am the sacred voice of my soul.
I am choreography on repeat and I am the
freestyle leading my way home.

I am a frequency. I am aligned.
My heart is beating through all space & time.
I am the love who is vibrating higher.
I am the light who is shining on brighter.

The person

I am the colours. I am the skin.
I am all of the DNA codes that I carry within.

I am the freckles, the scars, the tattoos and my
jewelry. I am the clothes, the style but most of
all I am the attitude.

I am a unique person.
I am a star up in the sky.
An imperfect astrological organization of me,
myself and I.

The witch

I am passion. I am fire.
I am the action that I take.
I am so unstoppable, motivated and empowered
that everywhere I go it will cultivate

I am the source. I am the muze.
I am that crazy thought who won't go away.
I am the thinker, the maker, the trouble and only
because they couldn't burn me at the stakes.

I am the teacher and the student.
I am the silence for God knows how loud.
I am the herbs, the trees & the medicine.
I am that voice who will tell you I'm proud.

The father

I am the sky, the wind, the birds and the leaves. I am the observer & through all eyes I can see.

I am the height. I am the fall.
I am that leap you take into faith.
I am unforgettable like a star falling the other way.

I am the signs. I am the universe.
I am all & all is me.
I am everything and yet I am nothing.
Another soul who's broken free.

The experience

I am the wise one. I am the fool.
I do my best in everything I do.
I am the insight. I am the question.
All that I need is what I have in the present.

I am the records. I am the downloads.
I am the listener, the speaker and the
microphone.

I am the truth. I am the river.
I am that pizza you don't want getting delivered.

The feather

I am ancient. I am new.
I am the earth and the cycles it goes through.

I am brave and I am wild.
I am the father and the mother of an invisible child.

I am three and I am two.
I am that friend who will always cuddle you.
I am here and I am now.
So it doesn't matter where you will go.

The mother

I am the one who will sing you to sleep.
I am the sound and the sweet melody.
I am the one who will kiss you goodnight.
I am the warmth, the blanket and your cute little
light.

I am the scent, the voice and the feeling.
I am the home you can always retrieve again.

I am the world, the heaven and gateway. Shifting
my shape to create something amazing.

The shadow

I am the woods. I am the whispering.
I am the fall of a branch on your back.
I am the footsteps. I am the following.
I am the voice who will tell you there's no way
back.

I am the flashlight. I am the grass.
I am the heartbeat pounding in your throat.

I am the butterfly. I am the scarabee
Realizing what I am truly worth

The cycle

I am the sunset. I am the dawn.
A bunch of muscle movement in between.

I am the tides, the seasons and the weather.
I am all simultaneously.

I am more of a night owl than I am a daydream
but always a rainbow. I am that pot of gold.

I am a dance, a moon phase and the never
ending story.

Be brave is what she said, be bold!

The south

I am the lion. I am the high priestess.
I am the magic, the power and the succes.
I am the rocks they have thrown at me and the
pyramid I build with it.

I am the purity, rebirth & skin.
I am the royalty, the divinity within.

I am the maps, the car and the road. The animal
crossing and that breeze through your hair.

I am that sing along to the radio.
A beautiful memorie in the garden of flair.

The flame

I am merely the lipstickprint on a glass I leave
behind, the ashes of a love spell and an
unspoken word.

I am the crystal ball.
I am the 'How do you know?'
I am the practice. I am the perfect.
I am the theory that was already inside of me.

I am the leaving without being gone.
I am unforgettable and I am irreplacable.
I am the plan you never saw coming.

I am the rose. I am the thorn.

The lesson

I am the key. I am the door.
I am the heart. I am the mind.
I am the mountain. I am sure.
That little girl I leave behind.

I am the waterfall. I am the sunshine.
I am the green, the blue and the purple.
I am chemistry. I am out of line.
I live inside my home like a turtle.

I am the past, the present and the future.
I am everything and yet nothing to become.

I am you. I am the world.

Bust most all I am.

The pie

I am the treasure. I am the chest.
I am the oyster. I am the pearl.
I am this wanderer on a queeste and his vanilla
chocolate swirl.

I am the gift. I am the talent.
I am the work that I put in and Im the cherry on
the top.

I am delicious. I am magnificent.
I am the blood, the sweat and the tears.

The vampire

I am whatever I want to be.
Unapologetically & fiercely.

I am the self who is putting me first and I am the
one knowing what it is truly worth.

I am the time. I am the energy.
I am the investment I make and I am the
decision.

I am the sand. I am the footsteps.
A touch of journey.

The inspiration

I am the impossible. Lucky number seven
making childhood dreams come true.

I am the compatible.
The perfect meeting in a dream.

I am the ideas. I am the suggestion.
I am the 'What if it's all going to work out just
fine?'

I am the failure and I am the completion.
I am the one who is not going to leave it at 'I
tried'

The conversations

I am the peace. I am the calmth
I am the white lotus.

I am the beauty and I am the pain.
I am the thoughts in my mind that seem to have
no shame.

I am the program and I am the programmer.
I am the observer running through the maze.

I am the allowance. I am the surrender.
I am the mud in which I grow.

The woman

I am too much and still too less.
I am the learning. I am the comfortable.
I am the wicked race but still the slow and
steady.

I am the cocoon. I am the butterfly.
I am the nectar of a mango.
I am the stranger passing by offering you a ride
home.

I am the tango.

The alarm

I am the warrior.
I am the light.
I am the elements, the ankh and a sexy ass woman.

I am grateful. Truly grateful.

I am happy to be me.
I am here. I am now.
I am everywhere, free and bound.

I am grateful. Truly grateful.

I am love.

The freedom

I am who I am.
Everything and nothing

I am what I choose.
Rainbows and butterflies.

I am the best part, the start and the end.

I am all and all is me.
Another soul who has broken free.

9 789357 447249